STEP-by-STEP

GEOGRAPHY

Maps and Globes

Sabrina Crewe

Illustrated by Raymond Turvey and Shirley Tourret

W

FRANKLIN WATTS

LONDON • NEW YORK • SYDNEY

© 1996 Franklin Watts
This edition 1998
First published in Great Britain by
Franklin Watts
96 Leonard Street
London
EC2A 4RH

Franklin Watts Australia
14 Mars Road
Lane Cove
NSW 2006
Australia

ISBN: 0 7496 2395 0
10 9 8 7 6 5 4 3 2
Dewey Decimal Classification 912
A CIP catalogue record for this book is available from the British Library
Printed in Dubai

Planning and production by The Creative Publishing Company
Designed by Ian Winton
Edited by Patience Coster
Consultant: Keith Lye

Photographs: The Image Bank: page 5 (Stephen Wilkes); NASA: page 25; Robert Harding Picture
Library: page 28 (Mike Agliolo); Tony Stone Worldwide: page 20 (John Lawrence); ZEFA: page 24.

Contents

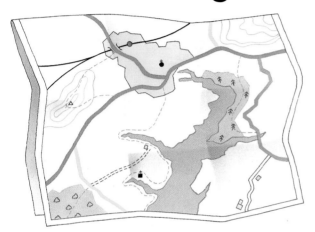

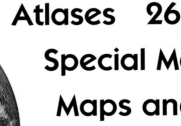

What are Maps?

Maps are drawings of places, seen from above. Imagine you are in an aeroplane, flying over your house. You can see where your house is in the street. You can also see the other streets and houses near where you live.

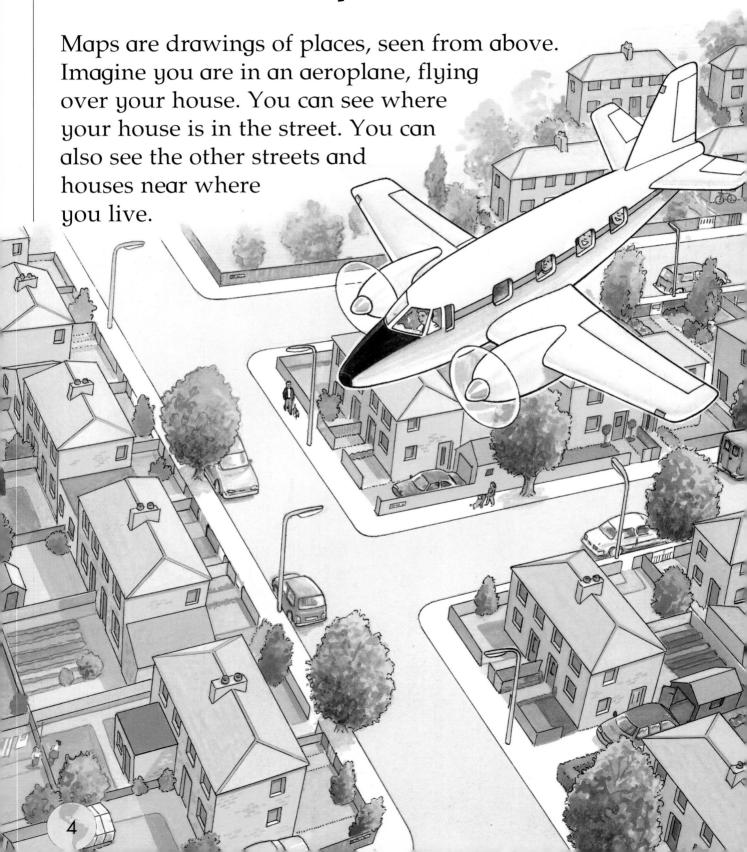

Maps can show a big **area**, such as a whole town or country, on a small piece of paper. They tell us where things are and help us find our way. This is a map of the streets in the picture opposite.

PARK STREET

ORCHARD ROAD

POND STREET

Maps can show us the whole world, too. A round map of the world is called a **globe**. Globes show us how the world looks from a spaceship.

Making a Plan

Try making a **plan** of something you know, like your table at home or at school.

Look at the things on this table. You can see them all outlined in the plan below the picture.

The plan is a map of the table. It shows where everything is.

You could make a map of your room to show a friend. Remember that a map is a picture drawn from above. First draw the shape of the room. Then mark where the door and windows are. Now put in your bed and the other furniture.

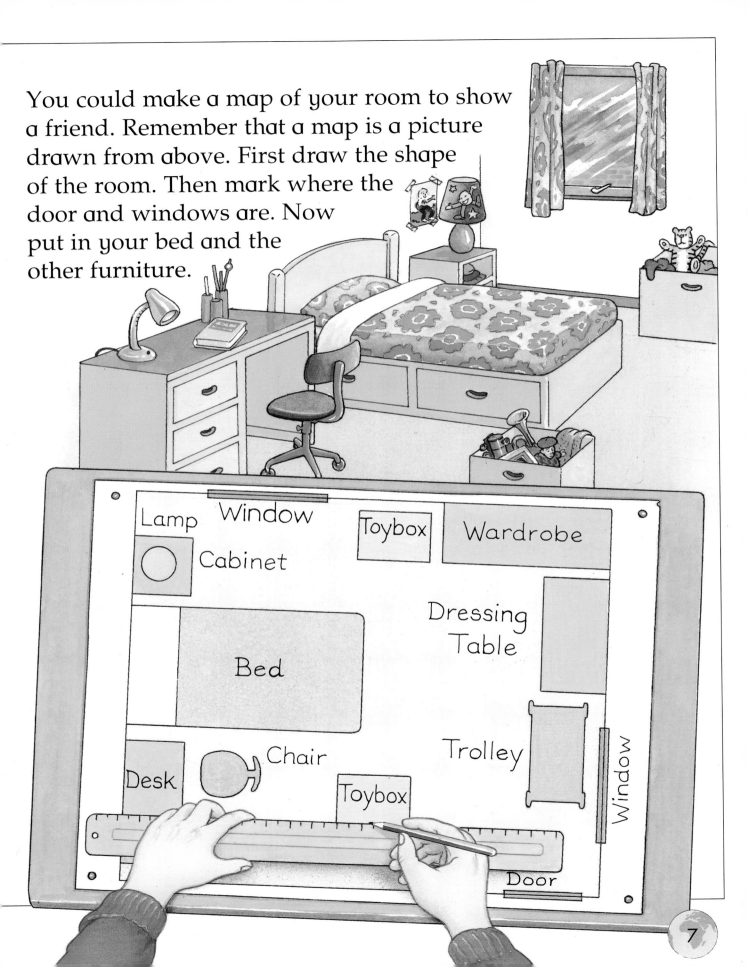

Symbols and Keys

Symbols are little signs on a map. Many maps use symbols to show where things are.

On this map, the purple symbols stand for shops. The grey lines are roads. The blue wavy line is a river. All of these are symbols. What other symbols can you see?

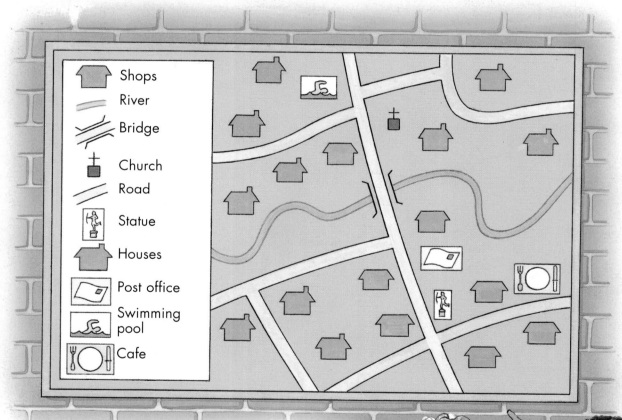

The list on the side of the map is called a 'key'. This tells you what the symbols mean. What does the knife-and-fork symbol mean? (Answer on p.32.)

Draw a map of an island like the one in this picture. Think about the things you can see on the island. What symbols would you use to show these things? Make a key with symbols for your island map.

Using Colours

Look at this map of a park. Colours are used to show what the different parts are.

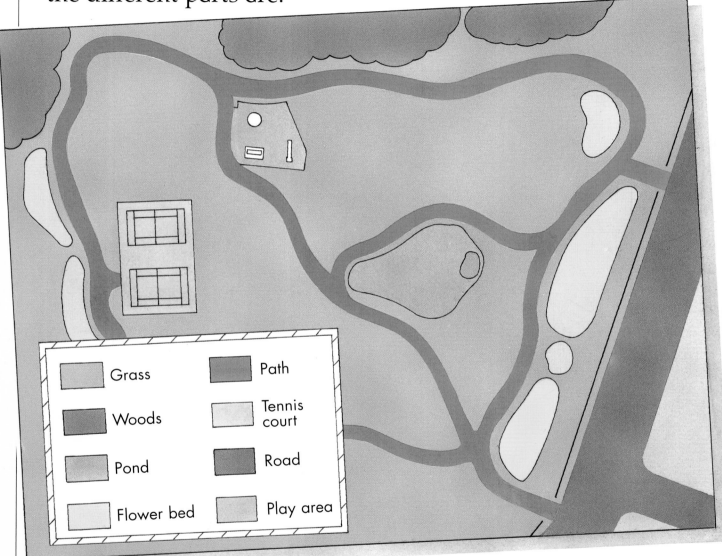

The key tells us that the light green areas are grass and the dark green areas are woods. Blue is used for the pond and pink for the play area. Look in the key for more colours. What do yellow and red stand for? (Answer on p.32.)

Make a map of your garden, or a park near you, using colours to show what things are.

On this tourist map, colours and symbols are used together. The colours show where the land and sea are. The symbols show us places that are fun to visit.

Which Direction?

While a map can tell you where things are, you also need to know which **direction** to travel in. We go in different directions to get to different places. There are four main directions: north, south, east and west.

This is a **compass**. It tells you which direction you are facing. A compass has a needle that always points north. If you face north too, then south is behind you; west is on your left and east is on your right.

MAKE A COMPASS

1 Ask an adult to help you with this project. Stroke a sewing needle with a magnet about 50 times. Stroke the needle in the same direction each time. This will make the needle magnetic.

2 Cut a circle of thin cardboard. Balance the needle on this and float it in a saucer of water. The needle will move round until it points north.

Maps are usually made with north at the top and south at the bottom. Imagine you are on the bridge in this map. Which direction would you go to get to the mountain? If the farmer's dog is by the pond, which direction must it go to get back to the farm? (Answer on p.32.)

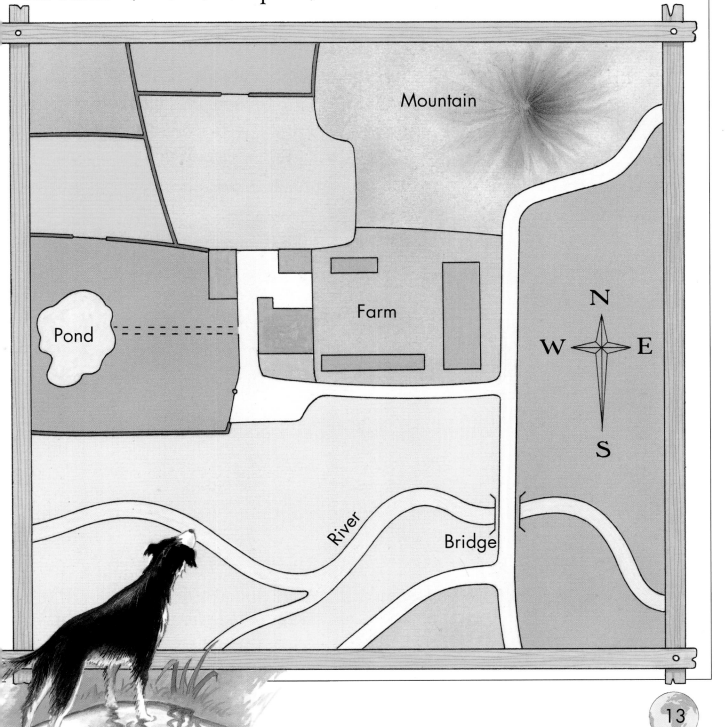

Following a Route

We all use a route to get to the places we want to go.

Vicky lives at 21 Cherry Tree Lane. Ben has asked Vicky round to his house at 4 Willow Drive. To get there, Vicky turns left out of her gate and right at the end of the lane into Park Street. She walks past the shops and turns left at the library into High Street. She passes the playground then turns right into Willow Drive. Ben's house is next to the church.

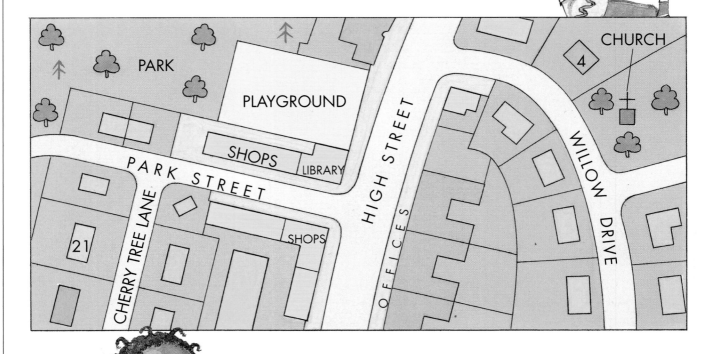

Make a map of the route you take when you walk to a friend's house. Write down directions so that someone else could use your map to find their way.

Somewhere on this map there is some buried treasure. Can you find it? Follow the directions to the secret hiding place.

Land your boat on Barnacle Beach. Go east until you reach Hopscotch Hill. Go north to the bridge, cross Raging River, and turn west. When you reach Wiggly Woods, find the path that leads south to Captain's Cave. Inside the cave there are two secret tunnels. Take the one that goes west. Come out of the tunnel and turn north. Stop at the wishing well and look east. Can you see the treasure next to a rock?

Where am I?

Some maps have lines that cross each other to form squares. These squares make a **grid**. A grid is very useful if you want to tell somebody exactly where to look on a map. Each square can be named by a letter and a number.

Imagine that you've just arrived at the zoo. You want to find out where the ostriches are.

If you look at the key, you'll find that the ostriches are in square **B2**. Put one finger on the letter **B** at the side of the map. Now put another finger on the number **2** at the top. Bring your fingers together in straight lines until they meet at the ostriches.

KEY

Butterfly house	E5
Crocodiles	B5
Elephants	A1
Giraffes	E4
Insect house	C1
Kangaroos	A3
Lions	C4
Monkeys	A5
Ostriches	B2
Pandas	E1
Penguins	D2
Sea lions	D4
Snakes	A4

YOU ARE HERE

Which square are the pandas in?
What can you see in **D4**?
(Answer on p.32.)

How Far Is It?

Maps are much smaller than the places they show. But they can still tell you the real size and **distance**. The places shown on maps would not fit life-size on to a piece of paper, so maps are always drawn to **scale**.

Most maps have a **scale bar** so that you can work out how big things are and what the distance between them is.

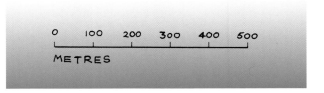

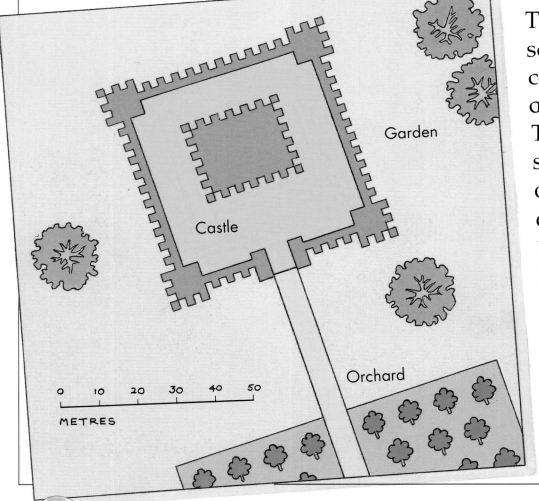

This is a large scale map. You can see a castle and a garden. The scale bar shows us that one centimetre on this map is 10 metres in real life. What is the distance in metres from the castle gate to the orchard? (Answer on p.32.)

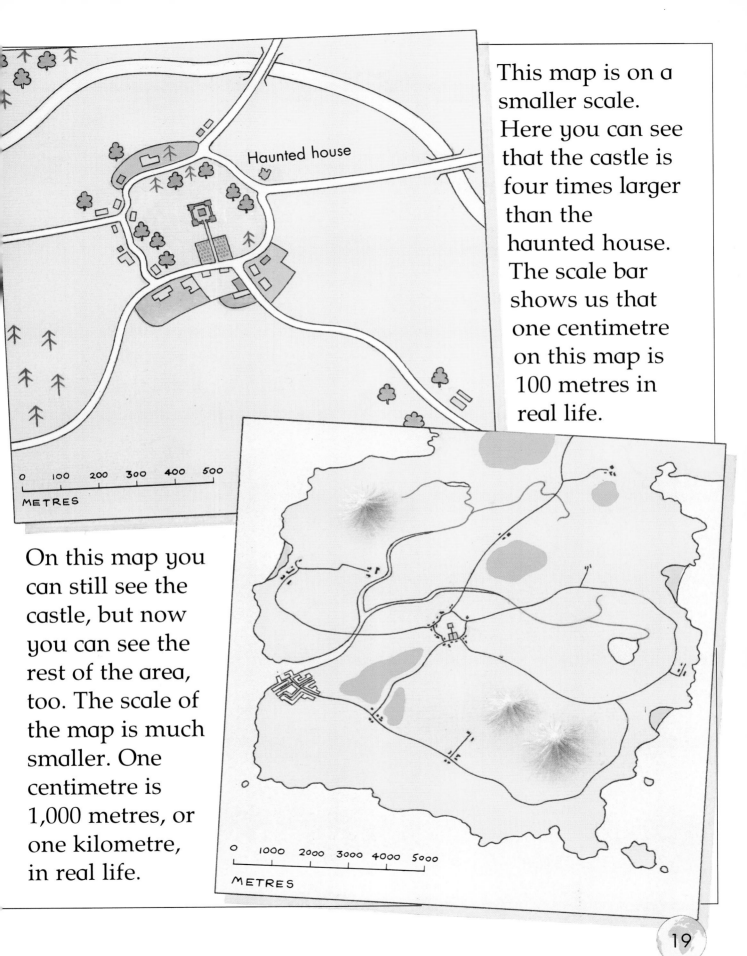

Haunted house

0   100   200   300   400   500
METRES

This map is on a smaller scale. Here you can see that the castle is four times larger than the haunted house. The scale bar shows us that one centimetre on this map is 100 metres in real life.

On this map you can still see the castle, but now you can see the rest of the area, too. The scale of the map is much smaller. One centimetre is 1,000 metres, or one kilometre, in real life.

0   1000   2000   3000   4000   5000
METRES

Maps for Different Things

This is a walking map. It is full of information for people who are interested in exploring the area on foot.

The lines on this map tell you many different things. They show footpaths and tracks through woods. They show roads and railway lines.

The red lines on this map of South America cannot be seen in real life. They mark the **boundaries** between countries. This map doesn't help you to get around, but it is very useful for learning about other places in the world.

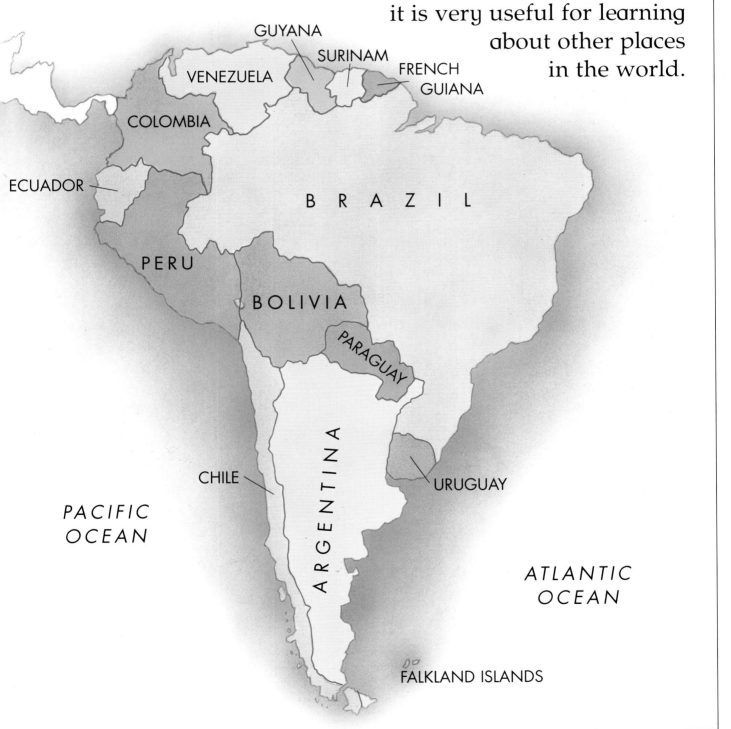

GUYANA

SURINAM

VENEZUELA

FRENCH GUIANA

COLOMBIA

ECUADOR

B R A Z I L

PERU

BOLIVIA

PARAGUAY

CHILE

A R G E N T I N A

URUGUAY

PACIFIC OCEAN

ATLANTIC OCEAN

FALKLAND ISLANDS

City Maps

Big cities can be hard to find your way around.

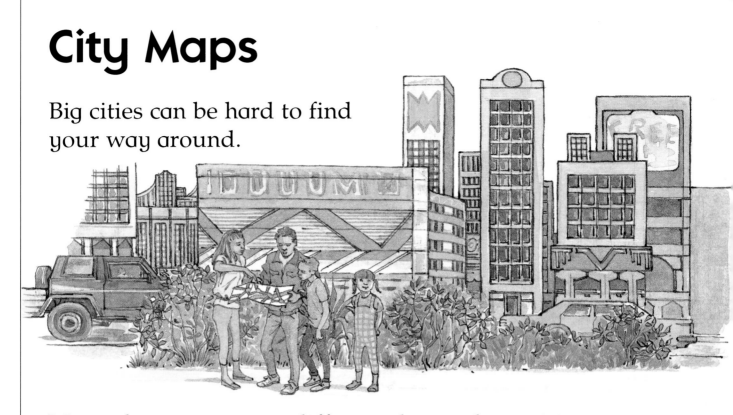

Maps show you many different things about cities. Look at these three city maps.

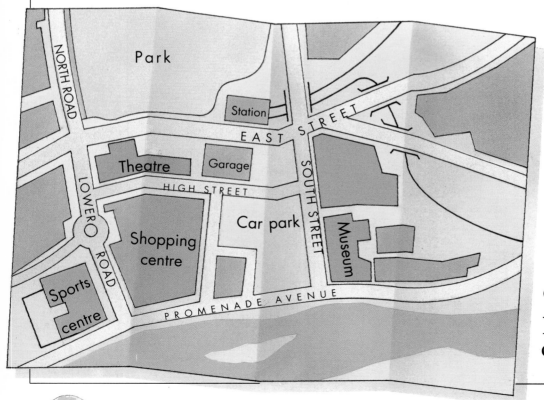

Some maps of big cities show every single street. These maps are useful for getting about town and finding particular places of interest.

This is a road map of the same place. You can see the whole city and all the major roads running through and around it.

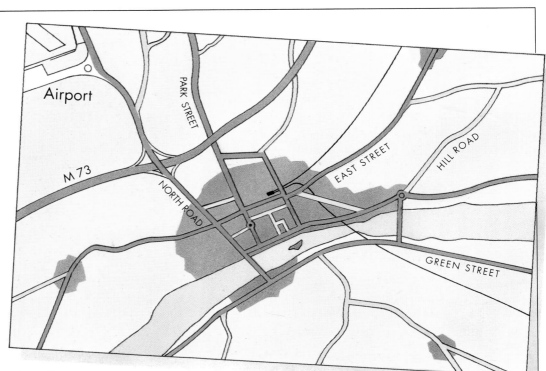

This map doesn't show any streets at all. It shows the route of a railway that runs under the ground. Look how the lines cross at some stations so that passengers can change trains to go in another direction. How would you get from Cross Street to Old Bridge? (Answer on p.32.)

CROSS STREET

HAPPY STREET

BROWN BRIDGE

CHURCH STREET

CASTLE STREET

GREY GATES

BROOK STREET

NEW ROAD

WINTER PLACE

ORANGE STREET

BLUE STREET

LAKE PLACE

WHITE ROAD

ABBEY LANE

MARSH STREET

OLD BRIDGE

POND PLACE

RED ROAD

MILL STREET

○○ CHANGEOVER STATION

STATION

EAST LINE

WEST LINE

NORTHERN LINE

CENTRAL LINE

How Maps are Made

Map drawing is called cartography. Maps have to be **accurate**, or they won't be useful. **Surveyors** work on the ground, measuring distances and gathering information for maps.

Cartographers use these measurements to draw maps on a computer.

Aerial photographs are pictures taken from aircraft in the sky. They show the world from above, just like a map. Aerial photographs are very useful to cartographers.

Satellite photographs are taken from space. They are useful because they show whole countries and **continents**. Can you see Africa in this satellite photograph of the Earth?

Atlases

An atlas is a book of maps. This world atlas has maps of every continent, ocean and country in the world. Each page shows a different area.

ATLAS
OF THE WORLD

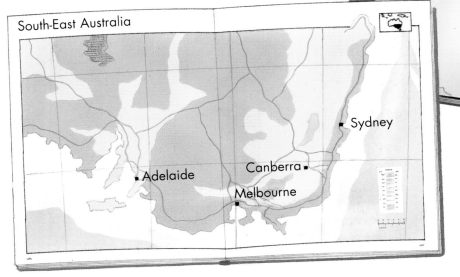

South-East Australia

Sydney

Canberra

Adelaide

Melbourne

This atlas is open to show part of the country of Australia.

A road atlas shows all the roads in a country. It is very useful for working out routes. Some people use a road atlas every day.

Some atlases are about things that happened long ago. Others show where different animals live.

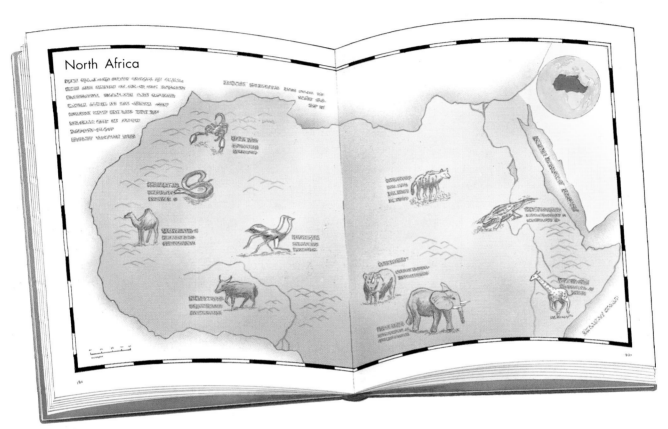

Every place or thing in an atlas is listed in the **index**. The index tells you where to find the place you are looking for.

Special Maps

Can you see what is special about this map? It is called a **relief map**. It shows how high and low the land is. You can see the mountains and plains.

This picture shows how undersea maps are made. Ships use special equipment to measure the depth of the water. This way they can work out where the hills and valleys are and make a map of the ocean floor.

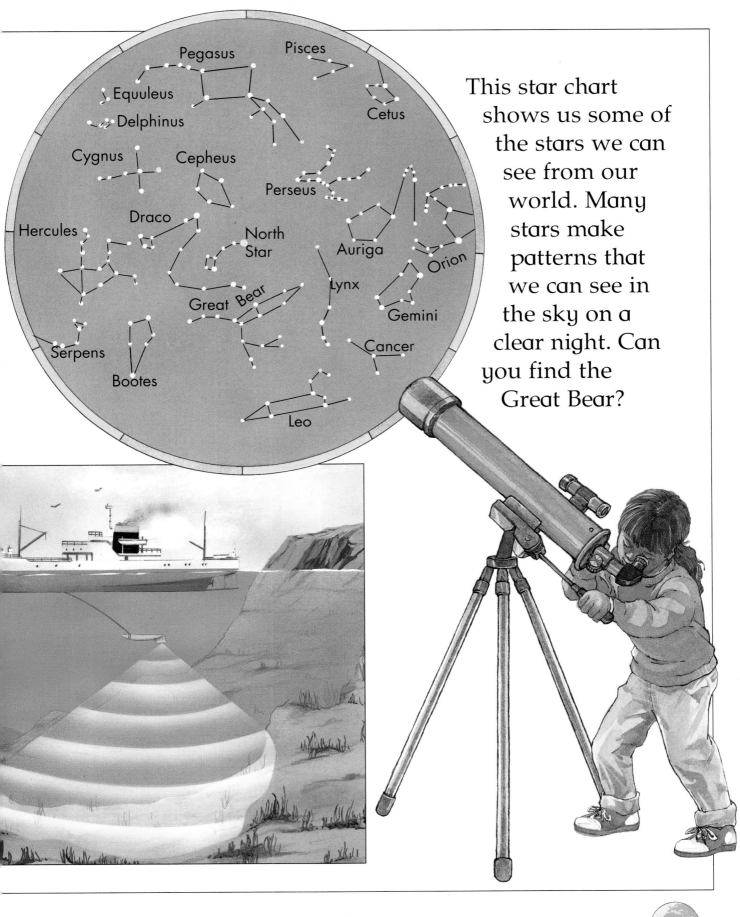

This star chart shows us some of the stars we can see from our world. Many stars make patterns that we can see in the sky on a clear night. Can you find the Great Bear?

Maps and Globes

There is only one way to show the world on a map just as it is in real life. The world is round, and so the map must be round too. These round maps are called globes.

Many maps and globes have **latitude** and **longitude** lines. Just like grids, these lines divide the world into pieces to help people find places.

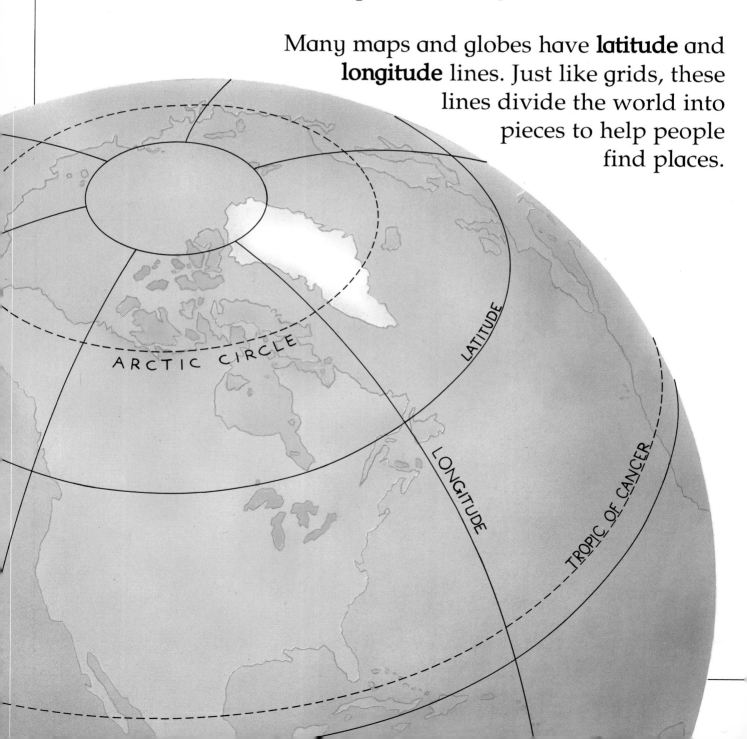

When we go somewhere new, we use a map to find our way. You need a map...

in the town...

in the country...

even indoors!

Without one, you might get lost!

Glossary

Accurate: Free from mistakes
Area: A space, or piece of ground
Boundaries: The limits or borders of an area
Cartographer: A person whose job is to design and draw maps
Compass: A tool used for showing direction
Continents: The main large land areas of the Earth
Direction: The way to go to get to a certain point
Distance: The space between two points
Globe: A round model of the world
Grid: A system of lines used for finding places on a map
Index: A list at the end of a book, showing what is in the book and the page it appears on
Latitude: Distance measured north or south of the Equator
Longitude: Distance measured east or west of an imaginary line called the Greenwich Meridian
Plan: A map of a small area
Relief map: A map that shows high and low ground
Route: A road, or way, for travelling
Satellite: A man-made object rocketed into space to go around the Earth
Scale: The size of a map in relation to the area it shows
Scale bar: A measured line used for measuring scale
Surveyor: A person whose job is to study and measure areas of land for map-making

Index

Answers

page 8 The knife-and-fork symbol stands for a cafe.
page 10 Yellow stands for flower beds and red stands for paths.
page 13 You would have to travel north to get to the mountain. The dog would have to travel east to get back to the farm.
page 17 The pandas are in E1. The sea lions are in D4.
page 18 It is 40 metres from the castle gate to the orchard.
page 23 Route 1: take the East line from Cross Street. Change at Pond Place for the Central line west to Old Bridge. Route 2: take the West line south to Marsh Street. Change to the Northern line up to Winter Place. Change to the Central line for Old Bridge.